THIS LAND CALLED AMERICA: RHODE ISLAND

CREATIVE EDUCATION

Published by Creative Education
P.O. Box 227, Mankato, Minnesota 56002
Creative Education is an imprint of The Creative Company
www.thecreativecompany.us

Design by Blue Design (www.bluedes.com)
Art direction by Rita Marshall
Book production by The Design Lab
Printed in the United States of America

Photographs by Alamy (Avico Ltd, Bill Brooks, James McClean, Mira, North
Wind Picture Archives, John Pitocco, Stock Montage, Inc.), Corbis (Bet-
tmann, Franz-Marc Frei, Peter Harholdt, Catherine Karnow, Kelly-Mooney
Photography, Bob Rowan/ Progressive Image, Tom Stewart, Shawn Thew/
epa, Onne van der Wal), Dreamstime (Vinoverde), Getty Images (Oxford
Scientific/Photolibrary), iStockphoto (Denis Tangney)

Library of Congress Cataloging-in-Publication Data
Wimmer, Teresa, 1975–
Rhode Island / by Teresa Wimmer.
p. cm. — (This land called America)
Includes bibliographical references and index.
ISBN 978-1-58341-792-8
1. Rhode Island—Juvenile literature. I. Title. II. Series.
F34.3.W56 2009
974.2—dc22   2008009511

First Edition
9 8 7 6 5 4 3 2 1

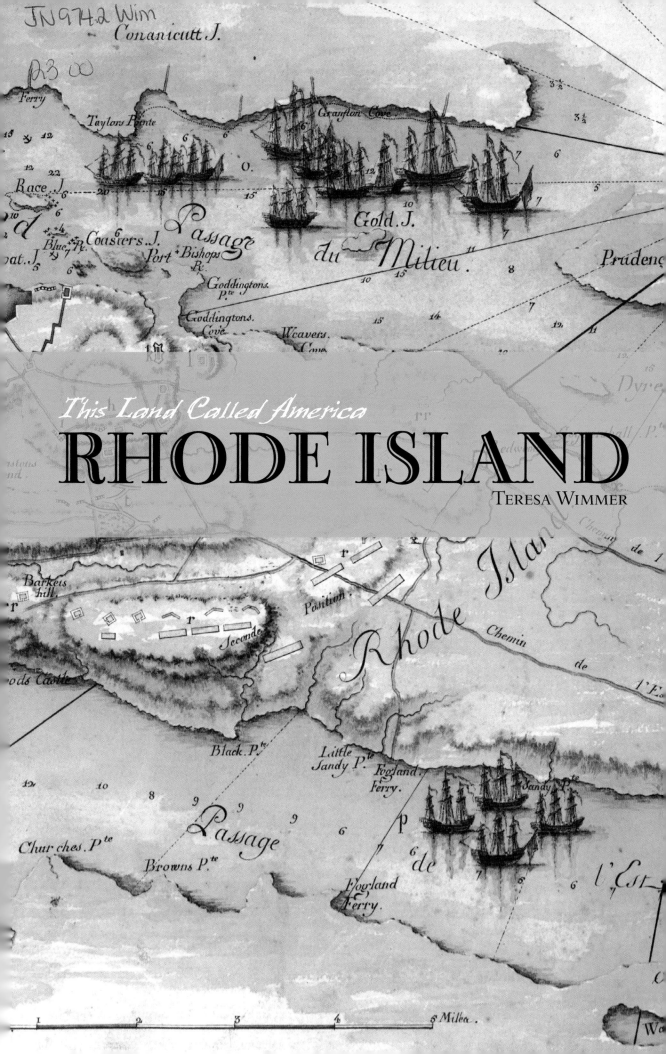

This Land Called America

RHODE ISLAND

Teresa Wimmer

Rhode Island

TERESA WIMMER

ON A BRIGHT SUMMER DAY, TOURISTS BOARD
A FERRY OUTSIDE THE TOWN OF NEWPORT,
RHODE ISLAND. SOON, THE FERRY BEGINS ITS
JOURNEY ACROSS THE SPARKLING WATERS OF
NARRAGANSETT BAY. ALONG THE BEACHES,
CHILDREN BUILD CASTLES IN THE WARM SAND. A
FEW PEOPLE FOLLOW A SANDBAR INTO THE BAY.
IT MAKES THEM FEEL LIKE THEY ARE WALKING
ON THE WATER. OFF THE COAST, FISHERMEN IN
A HUGE FISHING BOAT TOSS OUT A WIDE NET.
WHEN THEY BRING THE NET BACK UP, IT IS
FILLED WITH LOBSTERS. SEEING THE LOBSTERS
MAKES SOME OF THE TOURISTS' MOUTHS
WATER. THEY CAN ALMOST TASTE THE BUTTERY
SEAFOOD DRIPPING DOWN THEIR CHINS.

YEAR
1524   Italian explorer Giovanni da Verrazano sails into Narragansett Bay and names the nearby land Rhode Island.
EVENT

Land of Promise

INDIAN TRIBES SUCH AS THE NIPMUC, WAMPANOAG, NARRAGANSETT, AND PEQUOT LIVED IN WHAT IS NOW RHODE ISLAND. MOST OF THESE TRIBES LIVED CLOSE TO BODIES OF WATER. THEY FISHED IN THE RIVERS AND OCEAN WATERS AND HUNTED IN THE FORESTS.

In 1524, Italian sailor Giovanni da Verrazano landed on the coast of North America. He thought the place where he landed looked like the Mediterranean island of Rhodes, so he named it Rhode Island. Almost 100 years later, Dutch explorer Adriaen Block was the next European to explore Rhode Island when he came to trade furs with the American Indians.

In 1636, an English minister named Roger Williams traveled to Rhode Island from the Massachusetts Bay Colony to the northeast. He believed that the laws of churches should be separate from the laws of the government. Williams wanted to live in a place where he could practice those beliefs. He founded the town of Providence and the colony of Rhode Island on Narragansett Bay.

Other English settlers who wanted religious freedom followed Williams to Rhode Island. They established settlements and their own government, under the rule of England. At first,

More than 100 years after Giovanni da Verrazano (above) first saw the shores of Rhode Island, Roger Williams sought direction from the natives (opposite) there.

After the Gaspee was burned, King George III offered a reward for the capture of those who had led the attack.

State bird: Rhode Island Red

Gaspee burning

the Indians and white settlers lived peacefully and traded with one another. But, eventually, the settlers began to fight with and take land from the Indians. The fighting almost wiped out the Nipmuc, Mohegan, and Podunk tribes.

Throughout the 1700s, people and businesses in Rhode Island grew more successful. Farming, whaling, and sea trading became very profitable. Merchant ships sold and traded wood, salt, cider, dairy products, molasses, horses, and fish to the other American colonies and to Europe. Newport and Providence became two of the world's busiest ports for incoming and outgoing ships.

In the mid-1700s, England began imposing taxes on the American colonies to benefit the English homeland. All of the colonies, especially Rhode Island, began to rebel against the English. In 1772, a group of colonists from Providence and the surrounding towns boarded the English ship *Gaspee*, which had run aground in Narragansett Bay near Warwick. They set the ship on fire in an open act of rebellion against England, which led to the beginning of the Revolutionary War three years later. After the war ended in 1783, the colonies gained their independence and formed the United States. On May 29, 1790, Rhode Island became the 13th state to join the country.

YEAR

1636   The Providence settlement is founded by Roger Williams and later becomes the state capital.

EVENT

In the 1800s, textile mills for making cloth sprang up along the Blackstone and other rivers in Rhode Island. Mills that made metal tools and equipment were also built. Manufacturing and banking became important businesses. In the mid-1800s, railroads connected Rhode Island with other states. Trains carried farm products, manufactured goods, and people all around the country.

Many immigrants from Europe came to Rhode Island in the late 1800s. They worked long hours in the state's factories and mills. But by 1900, many textile mills began to move to southern states. The South's weather was better for growing cotton, and people there worked for lower wages. By the early 1900s, new industries such as electrical equipment and machinery manufacturing began to replace Rhode Island's textile mills.

Textile mills powered by the falling water on Rhode Island's rivers (above) provided jobs for the many families (opposite) who immigrated to the state.

YEAR
1708   The first census taken in Rhode Island counts 7,181 people.
EVENT

- 10 -

Small Wonder

RHODE ISLAND LIES IN THE NORTHEASTERN PART OF THE U.S. DESPITE ITS NAME, RHODE ISLAND IS NOT AN ISLAND. IT IS BORDERED TO THE NORTH AND EAST BY MASSACHUSETTS. CONNECTICUT FORMS THE STATE'S WESTERN BORDER. THE WATERS OF BLOCK ISLAND SOUND, RHODE ISLAND SOUND, AND THE ATLANTIC OCEAN WASH UP ALONG THE STATE'S SOUTHERN BORDER.

Rhode Island's geography consists of two land regions: the Coastal Lowlands in the eastern part of the state and the Eastern New England Upland in the western part. The Coastal Lowlands are lined with sandy beaches and are covered by saltwater ponds, marshes, and lagoons. The beaches are always changing. Every day, ocean currents and tides wash ashore and move sand from one part of the beach to another. Along the coast, seagulls, terns, osprey, and loons feed in the waters. Ducks, geese, and pheasants make their homes in the marshy areas.

Mackerels, sought for their oily meat, travel in large schools to feed on smaller fish near coastlines.

Many fish such as flounder, tuna, shark, and mackerel live in the waters of Narragansett Bay. The bay's shores are lined with rocky cliffs. These cliffs offer excellent views of the sparkling Atlantic Ocean. More than 30 islands lie in and around Narragansett Bay. On these islands, the forested land is softly rounded.

Of Rhode Island's 21 remaining lighthouses, 13 continue to operate, guiding boats safely to shore.

YEAR
1772   A group of Rhode Island colonists burns the English ship, *Gaspee,* in Narragansett Bay.
EVENT

To the west, the Eastern New England Upland region is covered by rolling hills, narrow valleys, ponds, and lakes. The hills of the Upland provide good soil for growing crops. Most of the state's farms are located there. Farms growing vegetables such as corn, tomatoes, and squash make the land look like a patchwork quilt. Orchards growing peaches, pears, apples, and berries also color the landscape. Nursery plants such as shrubs and Christmas trees are grown on Rhode Island farms and shipped to nurseries and flower shops around the country. The hillsides are also dotted with vineyards that grow juicy grapes for making wine.

The western part of the Upland region is covered by forests of oak, maple, hickory, and pine trees. The state's highest point, Jerimoth Hill, is in the far western part of the

The peaches (above) that are grown in the western part of the state make their way east, past forests and lakes (opposite), to be shipped from port cities such as Providence.

One of the Upland's major rivers, the Blackstone, provided power to Slater Mill in the late 1700s.

Upland. It is 812 feet (247 m) tall. People mine the hills of the Upland for natural resources such as sand and gravel.

Many of Rhode Island's major rivers, such as the Pawtuxet and the Blackstone, crisscross the Upland. This region is also the location of the Scituate Reservoir, a man-made pond used for storing water. The Scituate provides water for 70 percent of Rhode Island's people.

Not many people live in the Upland region. But people who love the outdoors enjoy fishing and canoeing in the area's many cool streams and rivers. The waters teem with fish such as trout, bass, and pike. Animals such as beavers and otters also make their homes on the rivers.

The weather in Rhode Island is milder than in most of the rest of New England. Each winter, the state gets about 39 inches (99 cm) of snow. Summers are usually hot and rainy. Strong storms and hurricanes often pound Rhode Island's coast in the summer and fall. The storms bring powerful winds and flooding.

Even on the coast, snowstorms are an expected occurrence during Rhode Island's long, cold winters.

YEAR
1790   The first successful cotton mill in the country is built in Pawtucket by Samuel Slater.
EVENT

Working and Playing

MANY DIFFERENT PEOPLE HAVE LEFT THEIR MARK ON RHODE ISLAND'S COLORFUL MAP. IN THE EARLY 1800S, IMMIGRANTS FROM IRELAND, GERMANY, SWEDEN, ENGLAND, AND PORTUGAL CAME TO THE STATE. THEY BUILT SHIPS AND FISHED THE OCEAN WATERS. IN THE LATE 1800S, PEOPLE FROM ITALY, GREECE, RUSSIA,

Poland, and Lebanon arrived. They worked in the state's many textile mills and manufacturing plants. In the 1950s, Hispanics and Asians came to escape poverty and war in their native countries and to make a better life.

Rhode Island natives of Narragansett heritage share their cultural traditions for occasions such as parades.

Today, about 80 percent of Rhode Islanders are white. About 11 percent are of Hispanic heritage. A smaller number are African American and Asian American. A long time ago, thousands of American Indians called Rhode Island home. Today, only about 5,000 remain. Some of the Narragansett

Mill workers of the late 1800s and early 1900s often had crowded but well-kept homes.

live on a reservation, or land set aside for them by the government. The reservation sits along the Pawcatuck River in the southwestern part of the state.

YEAR

1831   Silversmith and jeweler Jabez Gorham founds the Gorham Company in Providence.

EVENT

Rhode Island is the smallest state in the U.S., but more than one million people live there. That means that some of its cities are crowded. Almost 90 percent of Rhode Islanders live in major cities such as Providence, Cranston, Warwick, and Pawtucket in the eastern part of the state. But more people are now moving to the countryside and to small towns. Many of them drive to jobs in big cities. It takes less than one hour to drive from one end of the state to the other.

Many people in Rhode Island are involved in the fishing industry. Fishermen haul up 35,000 to 55,000 tons (31,752–49,895 t) of fish, clams, lobsters, and oysters from the salty bay waters every year. The seafood is then shipped to restaurants and grocery stores around the country. Although only about

The waterfront area of Providence (above) is much calmer than the stormy seas that commercial fishermen face (opposite).

YEAR

1888   Rhode Island becomes one of the last states to pass a law allowing men without property to vote.

EVENT

one percent of Rhode Islanders still farm, agriculture remains
an important industry as well. Agricultural products bring $25
million to the state every year.

Many Rhode Islanders work as doctors, nurses, teachers,
bankers, and retail assistants. Others work at the various
tourist sites around the state. Employees in Rhode Island's
factories make chemicals, plastics, electronics, scientific
equipment, machine parts, and toys.

*A view from the air
shows the fields that
produce Rhode Island's
agriculture (opposite),
while an indoor shot
captures the atmosphere
of a busy Providence
factory (above).*

In 1923, brothers Henry and Helal Hassenfeld started
selling textiles and school supplies in Providence. They named
their company Hassenfeld Brothers. A few years later, they
shortened the name to Hasbro. Soon, Hasbro branched out
to become one of the world's leading toy manufacturers.

YEAR

1914   Johnson & Wales College is founded in Providence.

EVENT

Rhode Island is also famous worldwide for its jewelry and silver products. In 1794, a Providence silversmith named Nehemiah Dodge invented a way to cover cheap metals with expensive metals to make them look nicer but cost less. Providence soon became the jewelry-making capital of North America. In 1831, Providence silversmith Jabez Gorham founded the Gorham Company to make silver spoons. Today, the Gorham Company is one of the world's largest producers of sterling silver.

As hard as Rhode Islanders work, they also make time for music and the arts. Composer and playwright George

YEAR

1938 The 1938 Hurricane slams into southern Rhode Island, its strong winds and tidal waves causing 311 deaths.

EVENT

Out and About

BECAUSE OF ITS BEAUTIFUL SCENERY AND OCEAN VIEWS, RHODE ISLAND HAS BECOME A FAVORITE TOURIST DESTINATION. IN THE LATE 1800S, WEALTHY NEW YORK FAMILIES SUCH AS THE ASTORS, THE MORGANS, THE BELMONTS, AND THE VANDERBILTS VACATIONED IN RHODE ISLAND DURING THE SUMMER. THEY BUILT HUGE, EXPENSIVE MANSIONS THAT OVERLOOKED THE COASTLINE. TODAY,

many people visit the Breakers, a 70-room summer retreat in Newport built by Cornelius Vanderbilt. Its rooms are filled with marble floors, crystal chandeliers, and gold-covered walls.

One of the best ways to see Newport and Rhode Island's other major cities is by walking. Newport's narrow Cliff Walk, a path that runs along the edge of steep bluffs, gives visitors broad views of mansions on one side and the Atlantic Ocean on the other. In the capital city of Providence, many people enjoy strolling along the footbridges, walkways, and green spaces of Waterplace Park.

North of Providence, in the city of Pawtucket, visitors can walk around the Slater Mill Historic Site, where Samuel Slater founded the first successful water-powered cotton mill in the U.S. in 1790. People can tour the museum to watch spinning and weaving equipment from the 1700s in action. Wilkinson Mill, also located on the grounds, contains a working 19th-century machine shop. Visitors can also marvel at the breathtaking waterfall that powered both mills.

In contrast to the humble marketing of local cotton manufacturers (above) were the grand showpieces of Newport's private mansions (opposite).

Each May and June, people flock to the east-central city of Warwick for another look at history. The celebration known as Gaspee Days marks the anniversary of the night when local colonists attacked the English ship *Gaspee* in 1772. The festival

YEAR

1978   The "Blizzard of '78" dumps 55 inches (140 cm) of snow on parts of Rhode Island.

EVENT

- 27 -

A 30-minute walk from the ferry station on Block Island brings visitors to the Southeast Lighthouse.

features craft fairs, dances, and delicious food. Many people camp out for the weekend to learn what military life was like during the Revolutionary War.

The town of Bristol in the eastern part of the state is home to the Audubon Society of Rhode Island's Environmental Education Center. The Center takes visitors on a guided tour of examples of the state's major wildlife habitats such as farmland, meadows, wetlands, and Narragansett Bay. Children can touch rare blue lobsters, fish in a 500-gallon (1,900 l) aquarium, and look inside a life-sized replica of a 33-foot-long (10 m) North Atlantic right whale.

Block Island is Rhode Island's southernmost point and lies in Block Island Sound. Each year, thousands of people take ferry or plane rides to the island to walk its nature trails, see its many historic buildings and lighthouses, and watch birds and other animals at the National Wildlife Refuge.

In addition to admiring Rhode Island's beautiful sights, people all over the state enjoy participating in outdoor activities such as horseback riding, hiking, biking, sailing,

Those who enjoy competitive sailing can race in the Swan American Regatta, held every two years in Newport.

YEAR

1996 A barge loaded with millions of gallons of oil runs aground off Moonstone Beach.

EVENT

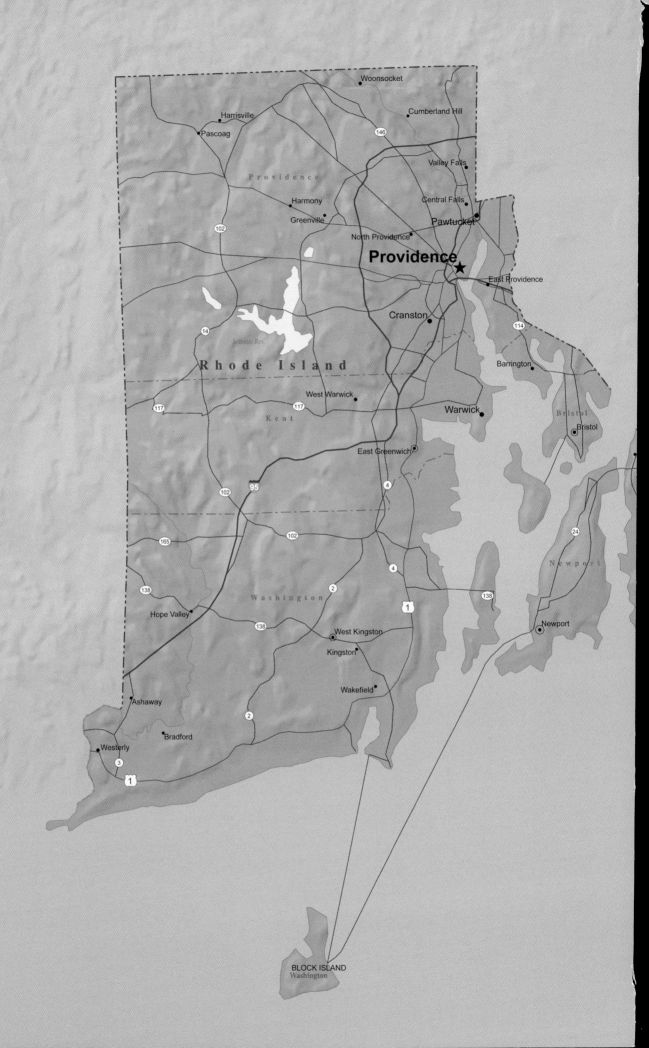

Woonsocket

Harrisville

Cumberland Hill

Pascoag

146

Valley Falls

Providence

Harmony

Central Falls

Greenville

Pawtucket

102

North Providence

Providence

★

East Providence

Cranston

114

Barrington

14

Seekonk Res.

Bristol

Rhode Island

Bristol

West Warwick

117

Warwick

117

117

Kent

East Greenwich

4

Newport

24

95

102

165

102

4

138

2

1

Hope Valley

Washington

138

West Kingston

138

Newport

Kingston

Ashaway

Wakefield

2

Bradford

Westerly

3

1

BLOCK ISLAND
Washington

QUICK FACTS

Population: 1,057,832

Largest city: Providence (pop. 172,459)

Capital: Providence

Entered the union: May 29, 1790

Nickname: Ocean State

State flower: violet

State bird: Rhode Island Red

Size: 1,545 sq mi (4,002 sq km)—smallest in U.S.

Major industries: fishing, manufacturing, farming, tourism

and fishing. They also enjoy watching sporting events. McCoy Stadium is home to the popular minor-league baseball team the Pawtucket Red Sox, better known as the Pawsox. Pawsox games often draw more fans than some major-league games. Rhode Islanders also pack the stands for the American Hockey League's Providence Bruins games.

With all there is to see and do in Rhode Island, it is no wonder that visitors keep coming back. They always find new places to explore. Rhode Islanders love their families, their freedom, and their land. And they are always eager to show newcomers the sparkling beauty of "The Ocean State."

YEAR

2003 The crowded Station nightclub in West Warwick burns down after a rock concert, killing 100 people.

EVENT

BIBLIOGRAPHY

Blanding, Michael, and Alexandra Hall. *Moon Handbooks: New England.* Emeryville, Calif.: Avalon Travel, 2007.

Curley, Robert Patrick. *Rhode Island: Off the Beaten Path.* Guilford, Conn.: Globe Pequot Press, 2007.

McLoughlin, William G. *Rhode Island: A History.* New York: W. W. Norton & Company, 1978.

Mobil Travel Guide. *New England 2006.* Lincolnwood, Ill.: ExxonMobil Travel Publications, 2006.

Moehlmann, Kristin, ed. *Fodor's New England.* New York: Random House, 2007.

INDEX